MARKETING

A How-To-Do-It Manual for Librarians

SUZANNE WALTERS

HOW-TO-DO-IT MANUALS
FOR LIBRARIES
Number 20

Series Editor: Bill Katz

NEAL-SCHUMAN PUBLISHERS, INC.
New York, London

Published by Neal-Schuman Publishers, Inc.
100 Varick Street
New York, NY 10013

Copyright © 1992 by Suzanne Walters

Printed and bound in the United States of America

Library of Congress Cataloging-in-Publication Data

Walters, Suzanne.
  Marketing : a how-to-do-it manual for librarians / Suzanne
Walters.
    p. cm. — (How-to-do-it manuals for libraries ; no. 20)
  Includes bibliographical references and index.
  ISBN 1-55570-095-0
  1. Public relations—Libraries—Handbooks, manuals, etc.
2. Libraries—Marketing—Handbooks, manuals, etc. I. Title.
II. Series.
Z716.3.W24 1992
021.7—dc20   91-45030
                                                  CIP

CONTENTS

INTRODUCTION

What is marketing? Is it just another word for sales, public relations, and advertising? Or is it something that encompasses these areas and goes beyond them?

Marketing: A How-To-Do-It Manual for Librarians examines marketing as a process through which we come to understand our customers. It enables libraries to be "market driven" or "customer driven." By using a marketing planning process we can understand just what our customers want—and how and where they want our services. As we go through the process, opportunities for growth and solutions to problems emerge.

To help librarians apply the benefits of marketing to their organizations, *Marketing: A How-To-Do-It Manual for Librarians* offers the kind of practical, step-by-step guidance that will take you from concept through development and specific implementation of a library marketing plan.

For libraries, our customers are not only the people who come to us seeking information, books, and materials; they are also individuals and organizations who have a stake in our organization. These stakeholders are the elected officials who control city budgets and our funding base, civic and neighborhood associations, and a wide variety of special interest groups.

Marketing applies to the development of both products and services. Libraries are primarily concerned with the provision of services. Service marketing differs from product marketing because services are often intangible, while product marketing generally depends upon tangible features. Service-oriented marketing also depends on building good relationships with customers and stakeholders. It requires the total commitment of an organization. All the staff members play a role in reinforcing the customer-service approach. This "market driven/customer driven" approach must be adopted throughout the organization in order to be successful.

Essentially, a marketing approach to services means that we talk to our customers, and that we develop specific products and services as a direct result of listening to their needs. The listening process stimulates creative solutions to problems. It drives an honest evaluation of current services and creates an awareness of changing customer needs. Marketing is also scientific: it involves accurate research, analysis, and systematic planning.

Adopting a marketing approach puts your library on the path to growth and vitality. When we are close to our customers, we can identify appropriate growth opportunities for the future. Our vision is supported by factual data, gathered through market research. These data can generate increased funding from the public and private sectors for libraries.

A marketing approach looks for opportunities to solve problems and create growth—characteristics that are inspirational to staff. However, the "market driven/customer driven" approach usually represents a complete change in service outlook for many libraries. Staff may consider a marketing approach to be "commercial" and manipulative, associating it with pressure sales techniques they've seen in advertising. While advertising is one marketing tactic, it does not define the marketing planning process.

There are two secrets to staff acceptance of the marketing concept, and they are crucial to success. The first is enlisting the full commitment of the executive director. This individual must totally adopt the concept of a "market driven/customer driven" institution and provide the necessary leadership to reinforce each aspect of the service. The second is the direct involvement of the staff. Staff may be hesitant at first. Why should they try to understand customer needs more clearly? It may seem laborious to understand the level of detail required for each target market. They may feel they already know what customers want. Planning takes time away from the desk and serving customers. However, when the staff is involved in the process of obtaining specific information concerning customers, they see their customers in a new and different light. This dedication and enthusiasm lead to greater commitment to the customer and improved service. A clear understanding of customer needs and measurements of customer satisfaction provide a factual basis for increased funding, whether from public or private sources.

The purpose of *Marketing: A How-To-Do-It Manual for Librarians* is to be a guide for librarians everywhere, helping them apply marketing principles to planning their products and services. Not only can such planning increase the effectiveness of library services, but it can also increase the value of the library as perceived by customers, elected officials, donors, and other stakeholders.

Chapter 1 begins at the beginning with developing a strategic attitude—which, for many librarians, may involve a shifting of perspective away from the view that marketing is a commercial tactic. It isn't. It's simply presenting the benefits of your organization to your various publics in an effective way. The next step is to develop a marketing plan for your library. This involves actions such as performing an environmental or situation analysis and targeting, or segmenting, your market. Also discussed are concepts like demand, competition, and the customer decision making process.

Chapter 2 covers the next step, market research, which includes such components as qualitative and directional research, primary and secondary information, focus groups, user surveys, and key dynamics of the marketing process, identifying problems and resultant opportunities.

Chapter 3 discusses how to position your library—to make sure the benefits of your organization are perceived by your clients. We suggest ways to assess your current positioning and strategies for improving it. We also discuss the concept of product life cycle as it applies to libraries.

Chapter 4 focuses on marketing strategies. It involves the four P's: product, place, price, and promotion. This chapter analyzes and discusses the role of each of these concepts and how each can benefit your library.

Chapter 5 discusses the pros and cons of marketing tactics. Included are public relations, advertising, direct mail, and telemarketing. Should you run public service spots on TV? Or choose a local radio station? Or simply develop a monthly book review column in your local paper?

Sample marketing plans round out the volume. Throughout *Marketing: A How-To-Do-It Manual for Librarians* you will find worksheets, charts, and diagrams to assist you as you develop your own marketing plan to best suit your own library.

1 DEVELOPING A PLAN

The first thing to do, before you begin planning, is to develop a "strategic mind set." In preparing yourself for the process to come, consider the following points:

Service cannot remain static: Products and services are constantly changing. For most people at the turn of the century, libraries were the only source for books and information materials. Now that books are easily available, libraries must make decisions on what products to offer.

Change is inevitable: Changes occur on a daily basis for libraries. New information products proliferate in the marketplace. Online technology is changing the way we do business. Budgets are shrinking; costs are soaring.

There is often a better way and the competition will find it: Libraries face competition for customers from a wide variety of sources, including newspapers, bookstores, television, and recreational activities. Indeed, new information delivery systems are becoming available through networking systems.

What is the difference between market planning and strategic planning? Strategic planning attempts to look five years or more into the future. It must be based on a clear insight into future customer needs. IBM is currently undergoing a strategic planning process to examine a move out of personal computers and into networking. Bell Systems throughout the country are undergoing strategic planning to position themselves in the information delivery business.

A marketing plan is a part of the strategic plan. The marketing plan identifies the specific strategies and tactics needed to create successful products and services within the strategic planning process. There are many different marketing plans within the strategic plan. A marketing administrative plan can be developed as an umbrella plan to identify the total "product mix" or "service mix" of the organization. The integration of all the services into one administrative plan provides strong guidance in determining action steps, integrating all products and services, and clarifying staff responsibilities.

A successful marketing approach depends heavily on the planning process. A service that is "market driven" is one that is based on the needs of the marketplace. Information about those needs is fundamental to successful market planning.

Before we can formulate a marketing plan, we must ask ourselves the following questions in order to define the nature and purpose of our organization:

- What business are we in? Are we in the informational business? The recreational or educational business? How do we decide our priorities?
- Who are we serving? Who are our primary customers? Are they children? Businesses? Adults learning to read?
- How well are we doing? What formal measurement tools do we employ to measure customer satisfaction? To understand customer needs?
- Who is our competition? Who else is providing services to these same customers? With whom are we competing for funding?
- What are our growth markets? What new products and services should we be developing to meet customer needs?
- What is our niche in the marketplace? Are there special niches that libraries are uniquely qualified to develop?
- What is the library's role in the information industry?

We can expect to encounter obstacles when we adopt a marketing approach. Some common ones are:

- *Resistance to change:* "We've always done it this way." Librarians often have difficulty giving up a product or service even though it is no longer needed. Market research provides the information you will need to encourage positive avenues of change.
- *Inability to listen to customers:* Even though we think we understand what our customers want, we must develop a system that allows us to listen. Our customers can suggest remarkable ways to improve our services if we take the time and make the effort to listen.
- *Tradition:* Libraries are strong organizations with deep-rooted traditions that are hard to change. However, when we work closely with our customers and are open to change, we can develop new traditions of service that will reward the library handsomely.
- *Issues of "the mission":* Often, a library's mission is too broad. Many libraries strive to meet the informational,

educational, and recreational needs of the community. But, for the library to be effective, its mission must be specific and focused. We need to examine our mission and to identify the role we alone can do well.

- *Being honest with yourself:* Market research often provides us with information that demands change in the way we provide services. However, it is difficult to be honest with ourselves and make the changes needed by our customers.
- *Acknowledging competition:* Although libraries tend to believe that they have no competition, there is in fact significant competition for funding. In addition, libraries compete for customers' time and with a wide variety of informational resources.

START WITH A MISSION STATEMENT

Every library must have a mission statement. It will help you understand the primary focus of your business and direct you to the necessary priorities and decisions. The more clearly your mission is stated, the easier it is to see marketing opportunities.

Traditionally, libraries have tried to be all things to all people. But in this world of diminishing resources and increasing sophistication, it is impossible to meet all of the needs of the customer. Libraries' missions will vary depending upon their location and their role in a public system, a corporation, or an academic setting. Branch libraries will differ from a central resource center.

The exacting process of developing an accurate mission statement involves determining the primary role of the library and establishing priorities for the audiences to be served and the services to be offered. It is an educational experience and should involve the board of directors as well as management-level staff. The development of a mission statement will require compromise. The Public Library Association has provided guidelines for the development of a mission statement in its publication *The Public Library Mission Statement and Its Imperatives for Service*, which offers a guide to ranking a library's products and services.

A powerful mission statement provides a strong direction for the institution. It provides clear direction for the marketing planning process. It should identify who is to be served. Can you express your mission statement in 25 words or less? How well is your mission statement understood by your board of directors? The staff? Your customers?

THE PLANNING PROCESS

ENVIRONMENTAL OR SITUATION ANALYSIS

In analyzing the environment in which you are providing your products and services, you might ask: What political/economic or environmental forces are affecting your institution? What growth elements are occurring in your service areas? What changes in population demographics demand your attention?

As a part of this environmental analysis, it is appropriate to do an "internal audit" of your library (see Figure 1-1). What are the strengths and weaknesses of your library? Almost all libraries feel as if they are understaffed and underfinanced. The marketing planning process focuses on problems and looks for ways to create opportunities. You may feel that you do not have sufficient staff to undertake a market planning process for all your services. Begin to develop your market-driven customer-driven approach with one service at a time.

DEFINE PRODUCT/SERVICE

Now you are ready to begin. Define the proposed product or service as you perceive it:

- Who wants your services?
- How much are they willing to pay for it? (What level of funding will be provided to support the service?)
- Who is your competition? Who else is offering a similar service? Who else will be competing for your customer's time?
- What will make the customer decide to use this service?

SEGMENTATION

Individual segments or target markets are described by using demographics. Demographic information includes age, sex, race, family size, number of children and adults in a family, educational level, income, and occupation (see Figure 1-2).

Individuals with similar demographic backgrounds may be quite different. For example, consider two 40-year-old adults with similar income and ethnic backgrounds. One may be married and have several children; the other might be unmarried or a single parent. One finds reading a stimulating hobby; the other prefers mountain climbing. Hobbies, interests, and other activities make up the lifestyle of these individuals.

FIGURE 1-1 Analysis Charts

ANALYZE YOUR ENVIRONMENT/SITUATION

Population Changes:
Economic Situation:
Political Situation:
Technology Changes:
Other Changes That Affect Your Library:

STRENGTHS AND WEAKNESSES OF YOUR LIBRARY

	WEAKNESSES	STRENGTHS
Administration/Board Structure		
Staffing		
Facilities		
Collections		
Funding		
Auxiliary Support Groups		
Other		

FIGURE 1-2 Demographic Information Targeting Senior Citizens

Demographics

AGE	SEX	INCOME	EDUC.	MARRIED	CHILDREN	RACE
55-57	65%-F	30,000	Coll.	35%		
58-60						
61-63						
64-66						
67-70						

Lifestyle

AGE:	55-57	58-60	61-63	64-66	67-70
Interests:					
Theater					
Gardening					
Activities:					
Golf					
Travel					
Bicycle					
Mobility:					

FIGURE 1-3 Identify The Demands Made Upon Your Library By Children In Each Segment:						
Age	0–1	2–3	4–5	6–7	8–9	10–12
Caucasian						
African American						
Oriental						
Hispanic						
Gifted						
Learning Impaired						
Living in certain area						
Single-parent family						
Working parents						
In day care ctrs.						
In Head Start						

FIGURE 1-4 Identify Program/Service Opportunities For Your Library

List segments to which the service will be targeted. (Do not make it too broad.)	Why was this segment selected?

Segment Selected	Demand	What sources did you use to determine demand?

We also include lifestyle information in our description of target markets. There are companies that focus on developing direct mail lists based on lifestyle information. (You can see the results of this type of targeting by looking through the bulk mail and catalogs you receive at home.) Define your segment or target market by demographics and by lifestyle.

The word *demand* refers to the total number of potential customers in a particular segment. For each segment we identified in the previous exercise, we must now identify the number of individuals within that segment. If we were to look at the various segments possible among children, we would identify the numbers of children by certain criteria, as shown in Figure 1-3. One might be age. We might also add a second criterion such as neighborhood location, or educational level of parents. In this way we can identify the demand for a product or service by segment (Figure 1-4).

Our next step is to identify the competition for the product or service under consideration. Competition can be direct. For example, in developing children's programs, we have competition from other children's activities. Indirect competition, on the other hand, results from such factors as competing for the parent's time to drive the child to an activity.

The simple chart in Figure 1-5 should be used for every product

FIGURE 1-5   Competition Analysis Worksheet

Competitor	Strengths	Weaknesses	Opportunities
1.			
2.			
3.			
4.			

FIGURE 1-6 Customer Decision Making Process

Program or Event	Time/date offered	Equipment or Staff Expertise	Price	Location of facility	Promotion	Customer Service	Comments, Incentives offered

FIGURE 1-7   Marketing Planning Worksheet

WHAT IS YOUR IDEA FOR A PRODUCT OR SERVICE?

_____

_____

WHAT SEGMENT OF THE AUDIENCE IS IT TO SERVE? (Remember to make this segment narrow.)

_____

_____

WHAT ADDITIONAL SEGMENTS WILL IT SERVE? WHY?

_____

_____

WHAT IS THE DEMAND FOR EACH SEGMENT THAT YOU HAVE IDENTIFIED?

_____

_____

HOW DID YOU DETERMINE DEMAND?

_____

_____

WHAT WILL INFLUENCE MEMBERS OF EACH SEGMENT TO USE THIS PRODUCT OR SERVICE? (In other words, what will influence the customer decision-making process?)

_____

_____

FIGURE 1-8   Market Planning Process

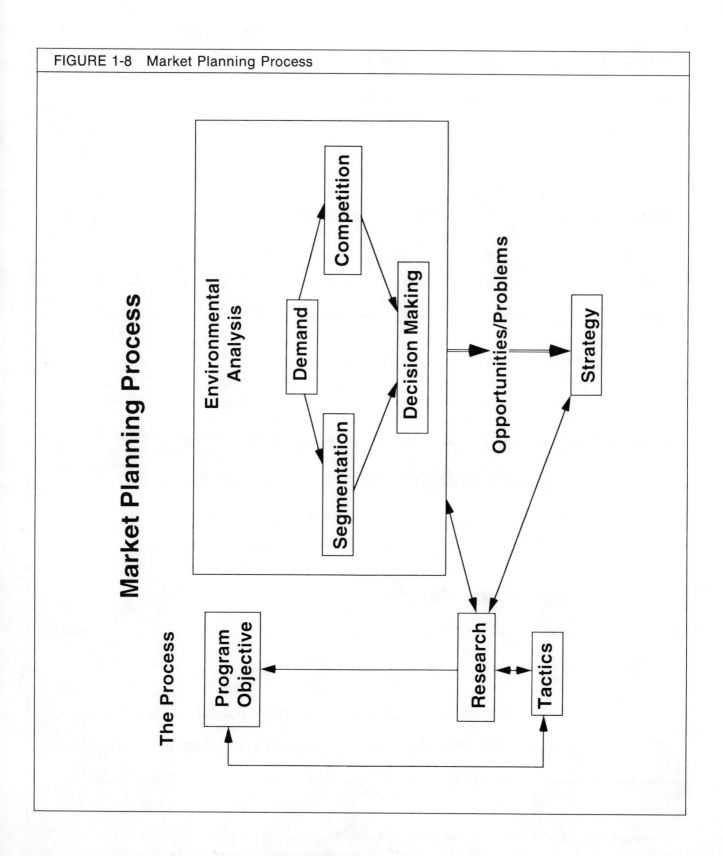

or service within the library. Make sure that you are thorough in your efforts to understand your competitors.

For libraries, competition comes from bookstores, newspapers, and television. When it comes to public funding, there is great competition from every other city agency. When identifying your competition for a specific program or service, identify all of your direct competition (bookstores, etc.) as well as your indirect competition (competing for funding, leisure time, etc.).

Next we must consider the consumer decision-making process of our customer (Figure 1-6). When we are working with pre-school children, the consumer making the decision to participate in the program is probably not the child. The decision-making process to participate more than likely resides with the parent or a teacher. As we are developing our market research plan, we must carefully consider what will encourage our potential customer, the child, to participate in our program or service. However, since the parent is the decision maker, what will convince the parent to provide the opportunity for the child to participate?

Let's examine some examples of the customer decision-making process. When you see an ad in the newspapers for strawberries for 25¢ a pint, it influences your decision to go to a certain store. Cereals designed for children are placed on the lower shelves so that children will see them and ask their parents to buy that brand.

What makes a customer want to participate in particular library programs. Is it the price? The day or time of the program? The ease of parking?

2 MARKET RESEARCH

Niche markets are those segments of the market that you have identified and decided you are uniquely able to serve. Often, as you examine your niche markets, you will find that you don't have enough information. You think you know what will attract consumers to use your service, but have no hard information to substantiate that feeling.

Primary and secondary information: The library is the best source for reference materials, periodicals, online databases, business and financial information, and census, demographic, and competitive information. Information that is already available is called secondary information. You did not have to create it. Even though it exists, this information may be very difficult to find. Be thorough in your search for qualitative and quantitative information through a variety of sources before undertaking to create your own data. In addition to libraries, tap local chambers of commerce as well as state and city offices.

Data that we must obtain through our own research efforts is called primary information. There is extensive methodology to use in designing primary research. There are two types of primary information—qualitative and quantitative. Qualitative research is research that we do to understand how our customers feel about the library, or how they feel about certain products and services. There are several ways we can obtain this qualitative information. Among them are personal interviews and focus groups. Through these efforts we can understand customer perceptions and behaviors. A common marketing adage is, "Perception is reality." We must make every effort to understand how our customers and potential customers perceive our products and services. But be prepared for surprises. For example, in using qualitative methods with minority populations, very sensitive issues that affect these customers' use of the library may emerge.

Qualitative research: Focus groups: Focus groups are among the most successful forms of qualitative research. This methodology is used when you want to understand how a group of individuals feels about a product or service. Focus groups are very useful in dealing with minority groups, neighborhood groups, children, seniors and business customers, even staff members. (See "A Room of Their Own," *School Library Journal*, February 1991.) A typical focus group consists of approximately 12 individuals (can be eight to fifteen) who represent a homogeneous segment. These people sit in no particular order around a table in a room. Their discussion is facilitated by a highly trained moderator, who uses a discussion guide that has been developed with input from library administrators and appropriate staff. The guide begins with a discussion of the library in general, moves on to more specific issues such as library usage, and continues into very specific issues as the discussion progresses.

It is preferable to hold focused group discussions in a facility specially designed for this purpose. Such facilities are available in shopping centers or at market research companies. Ideally, the facility consists of a conference room set up for the group discussion with a one-way glass separating the group from observers, who do not participate in the discussion in any way. The discussion is audiotaped and videotaped, so that market research professionals can review the discussion as they develop their analysis and report. Library administrators, staff, trustees, and other key individuals can listen to the discussion as they observe the participants' reactions to specific products and services and/or the library in general. As the participants provide insight into the library's products and services, specific issues and opportunities emerge.

Getting people to participate in a focus group requires a special effort. You might offer an invitation over the phone to a potential participant. Offer incentives. In commercial enterprises, those incentives are money. Within the library setting, incentives can come from various local merchants. For a children's focus group, get the support of the local amusement park, ice cream stores, and pizza shops. Children love prizes. Organize ethnic groups with particular care. Community leaders, local clergy, and other respected members of the community can be very helpful. Always communicate to the participants in writing and be sure to say, "Thank you" afterwards.

If the focus group discussion is to have validity with the participants as well as outside audiences, a trained facilitator from outside the institution is needed. Facilitators can be found through your local chamber of commerce, universities, and market research companies. Trained facilitators are not biased and can lead the group in a managed discussion. It is not appropriate for library staff to conduct the focus groups, since they are biased in their support and tend to try to convince the participants rather than listen to the customer.

Directional research: Being close to the customer is very important in the marketing process. Another way of gaining customer input is to simply make it a rule to talk to three customers every day. Ask if they got what they came in for; ask how you can serve them better. The responses will provide you with surprising direction information.

Other forms of directional research include short, written surveys. Examples that can be used within a library to provide insight into problem areas are found in Figures 2-1, 2, and 3. These surveys are not difficult to design and should be used frequently to identify customer issues. When they are passed out on a random basis, they are not quantifiable. However, they will certainly provide you with directional information.

Spending the money: How do you determine what to spend on market research? What is the cost of a mistake? Market research saves millions of dollars for corporations planning new products and services. If you are contemplating a major bond election, a few thousand dollars in market research is well worth the investment. Market research can determine the direction and communication strategies for a successful campaign. It can help you design a building that will meet customer needs. When planning specific programs, look at the cost of a mistake.

Focus groups usually cost $2,500 or more per group. Costs vary depending on incentives that are offered to encourage people to participate, the location, and the facilitator. Quantitative studies vary in price depending on methodology and difficulty of study.

Getting the help you need: Market research assistance can be secured through the small business area of your local chamber of commerce. In addition, many corporations have market research departments, whose employees may work with you on a voluntary basis. Look in your yellow pages for market research companies in your area. These companies might help you directly or contribute information. Local universities often have a marketing department. A close partnership with marketing professors and students can provide a wealth of information.

The three customer attitude and evaluation surveys in Figures 2-1, 2, and 3 may be reproduced and used in your library. The surveys should be handed to customers over a period of one week. They are designed to provide directional information, to give you an indication of a customer service problem. Additional research will provide more in-depth and specific information about problem areas.

Use market research to understand your specific segments, the demand for services, the customer decision-making process, and your competition.

FIGURE 2-1   Library Customer Attitude Assessment

Please place a check in the box that is appropriate.

Question	Strongly Agree	Agree	Disagree	Strongly Disagree
The library has the materials I need.				
It's easy to find the materials.				
Staff are helpful and knowledgeable.				
The computer catalogue is easy to use.				
It is easy to renew books and materials.				
The hours of service are convenient.				
Buildings are clean.				
It is easy to find a place to ready and study.				

Please circle your gender: Male   Female

Please indicate today's date: _____   and time:_____

FIGURE 2-2   Scale-Based Sample Evaluation

Please place a check mark at the appropriate location to indicate how you feel about library services. The plus side of the scale represents the highest mark. The minus side represents the lowest. For example, if the library has everything you need, place a "x" on the "+2."

STATEMENT: *EVALUATION*

The library has what I need.   +2 . . . . . 0 . . . . . −2

Reference services provided the answer I needed.   +2 . . . . . 0 . . . . . −2

The automated catalog is easy to use.   +2 . . . . . 0 . . . . . −2

Materials are easy to find.   +2 . . . . . 0 . . . . . −2

Signage and directions are very helpful.   +2 . . . . . 0 . . . . . −2

Staff are knowledgeable and helpful.   +2 . . . . . 0 . . . . . −2

Your Age: _____

Please circle: Male or Female

Today's date: _____

FIGURE 2-3   Computer Assessment Survey

Question	Strongly Agree	Agree	Strongly Disagree	Disagree
The automated catalog is easy to use.				
The directions for use are easy to understand.				
There are an adequate number of public access terminals.				
I want to print information directly from the computer.				
I want to check out books directly from the computer.				
The computer service is complex.				
I would like to renew books directly from the computer.				

Your Age: _____

Please circle: Male   or   Female

Today's date: _____

IDENTIFYING PROBLEMS

For libraries, problems usually center around money (very little), staffing levels, collections, technology, and customer service. The problems of a declining economy and increasing costs of books and materials challenge every library in the country. The situation forces us to look closely at our mission and the services we should be providing.

Take the time to analyze. First, think about a problem as a situation that needs correcting. Careful examination of a problem often leads to the discovery of an opportunity.

We often talk about "the window of opportunity." Before you develop goals and objectives, you must state your assumptions. Assumptions provide guidelines and rationale for crafting your goals. They describe your assessment of economic or environmental conditions that are beyond your control but that you must contend with as you carry out your plan. You cannot prove assumptions. They are based on the best information you have.

A declining economy and increased unemployment can create an opportunity for libraries. Individuals need information on career searches, job retraining, and resume development when there is increased unemployment. The library has an "opportunity" to respond to a problem. There may also be opportunities for additional funding through foundation grants, LSCA funds, or corporate funds to support this opportunity.

Creative problem-solving sessions with a small group of staff bring consensus and understanding. As you begin to discuss problems, look for opportunities. When those issues we identified previously come to the surface, question them.

When you hear: "We've never done it that way before."
Ask: "Why haven't we?"

When you hear: "We can't do it because of a lack of funds."
Examine alternative funding sources—for example, partnerships with business.

When you hear: "We've tried that before and it didn't work."
Ask: "Why didn't it work? What is different this time? What part of the project did not work?"

When you hear: "We don't have the time."
Ask: "How important is this project or service? What can be delegated to other individuals?"

FIGURE 2-4   Problems/Opportunities Worksheet: Problems

List the problems that affect your library:

1. Customer Service Problems

_____

_____

2. Technology Issues

_____

_____

3. Collection Issues

_____

_____

4. Funding Issues

_____

_____

5. Staffing Issues

_____

_____

6. Facilities Issues

_____

_____

FIGURE 2-4 Cont.   Problems/Opportunities Worksheet: Opportunities

1. Customer Service

   Enhance level of service to customers.

   Which segment? _____

   _____

   How? _____

   _____

2. Technology

   What opportunities exist to improve service through technology?

   _____

   _____

   _____

3. Collection

   What opportunities are there to share resources? Enhance collections?

   _____

   _____

   _____

4. Funding Issues

   Opportunities for bond elections, referendums, private funding, fee-based services:

   _____

   _____

   _____

FIGURE 2-5 Prioritization Chart	
Prioritize the Opportunities	Rationale Behind Prioritization

GOALS AND OBJECTIVES

After you have completed your information gathering on trends, demographics, and the economy, identified problems and opportunities, and analyzed the facts concerning market segmentation, demand, competition, and the consumer decision-making process, it is time to write goals and objectives.

FIGURE 2-6 Marketing Goals For One Year					
Service Goals	Funding Goals	Positioning/ Promotion	Facilities/ Locations	For Customers	Specific New Product or Service

Example of a goal with objectives:

GOAL: To develop a new preschool read-aloud program.

Objective: To reach 2,000 children ages three to five.

Objective: To serve four economically disadvantaged neighborhoods.

Objective: To raise $50,000 within six months to support the program.

Objective: To promote this program through 30 preschools and Head Start organizations.

As you can see, goals should be broad (Figure 2-6). They should be based on information gathered through your situation/ environmental analysis. You should have a separate goal and set of objectives for each segment, or niche, of the marketplace you have decided to target for your services. Some examples of readily quantifiable objectives are: market penetration, ticket sales, number of people in attendance, circulation measurements, and increased card registration.

Establishing specific goals and objectives provides very specific targets for which to aim. Having specific goals and objectives forces you to use data effectively, helps set priorities for activities, and gives you an idea of the resources needed to attain them. It also forces you to realize that some of your goals are unrealistic. Goals that encounter too many obstacles should be eliminated.

MARKETING OBJECTIVES

Objectives must be measurable and quantifiable. Identify target markets, promotional costs, and funding sources within each objective. Below, list your objectives for each goal category:

1. Service goal:
Objectives:
a.
b.
c.
d.

2. Funding goal:
Objectives:
a.
b.
c.
d.

3. **Positioning/Promotion goals:**
   Objectives:
   a.
   b.
   c.
   d.

4. **Facilities goals:**
   Objectives:
   a.
   b.
   c.
   d.

5. **Customer goals:**
   Objectives:
   a.
   b.
   c.
   d.

6. **New product/service goals:**
   Objectives:
   a.
   b.
   c.
   d.

3 POSITIONING THE LIBRARY

HOW IS YOUR LIBRARY PERCEIVED?

Positioning plays an important role in the development of marketing strategy. It provides a framework upon which to build.

Positioning is often called the battle for your mind. It is defined as the way a product or service, company or institution is perceived by the client, customer, investor, consumer, or voter. Positioning is achieved through advertising, promotion, and communication programs. How is your library perceived in your community? As a leading cultural institution? As providing important service to the community? Producers of food products ask themselves about positioning strategies when they examine their advertising budgets. Sugar-coated cereal, for example, is positioned as a product for children, so it is placed on the lower shelves of the grocery store and advertised on television at times children will be watching.

Libraries must be aware of their own position in the marketplace. Positioning refers to how your library is perceived by the various customers it serves, as well as local elected officials, community leaders, and stakeholders.

Corporations behind consumer products give a great deal of thought to positioning strategies as those strategies will influence how customers perceive their products. Think of Maytag Corporation. It has positioned its products on durability. J.C. Penney's has recently been repositioning its stores as an upscale clothier. You must position your library for each audience. Often that calls for specific strategies for each group.

Those audiences for a public library might include the following:

1. Elected officials who determine the library budget
2. Parents and children
3. The business community
4. Neighborhood associations
5. Senior citizens
6. Donors
7. Customers seeking popular materials
8. Students

In an academic library, audiences would include:

1. Administrators who determine the budget
2. Faculty members
3. Undergraduate students
4. Graduate students
5. Businesses that provide corporate support

In addition to positioning the library as a whole, position individual products and services. For example, providing an automated circulation system offers an opportunity to reposition the library. However, in promoting this new service, remember that it is not the automation that customers will think is important, but the benefits of that automated circulation system—such as faster access to books and materials and/or more accurate information about materials.

Each segment will require separate positioning strategies. An outstanding summer reading program can be used to position the library to parents and children.

Some libraries provide special services for elected officials. This targeted service serves as a positioning strategy for that segment of the market. Services designed to meet the needs of the business community position the library to that community.

The keys to position are communication, advertising, and promotion. If you establish a strong business department, but don't let the business community know, your positioning strategy will be ineffective.

QUESTIONS TO ASK

When positioning your product/service or library, ask yourself the following questions:

How do your audiences perceive you now?

- Mayor, city council, other elected officials
- Business leaders
- Parents and children

What programs/services will enhance the position of the library in the eyes of your audience?

- Special events? Sponsoring an authors series offers the opportunity to position the library to a select audience
- Philanthropic programs? For example, winning a National Endowment Challenge grant can be used to position the library in the eyes of prospective donors.
- Special communication programs?
- Special services? Automated circulation and delivery systems offer opportunities to position the library as a state-of-the-art organization.
- Special collections/exhibits?
- Organized lobbying efforts? Friends groups can be very effective in an advocacy role.

How can you use the media to communicate your position?

- The objective of public relations, publicity, and advertising is not only visibility, but also positioning. Communication through the media offers an opportunity to reinforce how your library is seen by the customer.

A solid, strong position in your community is not achieved overnight or through a single program. It comes through constant good customer service, quality products, and continued visibility.

POSITIONING/REPOSITIONING
Why is positioning or repositioning done?

- To react to a changing market. Libraries are in the midst of the changing marketplace of the information industry.
- To correct a damaged or weak posture. Budget cuts and other adverse financial conditions damage the library's position in the community.

MARKETING POSITION STRATEGIES
Strategies to improve the position of the library may include:

- Positioning on good customer service.
- Positioning on driver product attributes. Federal Express and the U.S. Post Office both position on delivery of their service.
- Position on distinct market segments like children's services.

The simple survey shown in Figure 3-1 helps determine what customers/voters feel is most important as well as what they look for. Individuals are asked to put a check mark in each box they agree with. The survey provides directional information for the development of a positioning strategy.

POSITIONING STRATEGIES
Successful positioning strategies must possess two important attributes. They must be unique and they must be credible.

The purpose of a positioning strategy is to create distinction in the minds of your customers between your library's product/service and other similar products/services. Unsupported claims to distinction do not work when promoting your service

FIGURE 3-1 Assessing Your Position: Market Research Survey

The Library:	Most Important	Everyone claims	I look for
is on the cutting edge of technology			
says a lot about a city			
has experienced, knowledgeable personnel			
provides good customer service			
protects photos and books about our history			
helps adults to learn and read			
is important for children			

Your age:_____   Please circle gender: Male   Female
Library:_____ (name branch)

****

to intelligent voters, customers, and politicians. You should promote only what you can deliver. A positioning strategy must have credibility.

THE POSITIONING STATEMENT

When you communicate your position to your audience, you do so through a positioning statement. State your message clearly in 25 words or less.

For example, the positioning statement for the Post Office overnight delivery service is "We deliver, we deliver . . ." Nordstrom's retail stores say, "No problems at Nordstrom's." The Denver Public Library's positioning statement for their $91.6 million bond election was "A Library Says a Lot About a City."

Develop your positioning statement: _____

_____

_____

_____

_____

CUSTOMER COMMUNICATIONS

Consider your library's brochures, letterhead stationery, and business cards. Are they consistent? Do they present the kind of image you desire? Do you have a logo that conveys the mission of the library? Are there graphic standards for the use of that logo and the design of your stationery, signage, and other elements of communication?

How about the signage at your library? Does it provide clear direction? Is it easily understood?

What image do your facilities, furniture, and fixtures present to your customers? Are they cluttered, disorganized? Do you have handmade directional signs? Does it look as though you are barely surviving economically?

Are your hours of service designed to provide optimal service to your customers?

All of these elements reflect the position of your institution in your community. They reinforce the image you project.

PRODUCT LIFE CYCLE

Every product or service has a life cycle. The product life cycle curve shown in Figure 3-2 applies to every product and service. The curve shows that products are most profitable during the growth stage. Where do you think libraries fit on the product life cycle?

Marketing-oriented businesses constantly monitor the life cycle of their products and services. Some products like Ivory Soap and Arm and Hammer Baking Soda have been at the mature point in their product life cycle for years. Both of these products have had a very long product life cycle. However, when sales begin to slip, a new advertising program appears to remind the customer of the benefits of these products. We, too, need to remind our customers of the library's products. In high-tech industry a product life cycle of 18 months is considered long. The computer hardware and software industries must constantly be updating and renewing products. Libraries as a whole have had long product life cycles.

All consumer-oriented businesses realize that they must constantly introduce new products and services to remain viable in the marketplace. Libraries must consider new products and services, too. What are those products for your library? Are they videotapes? Books-on-tape? CD-ROM and online information

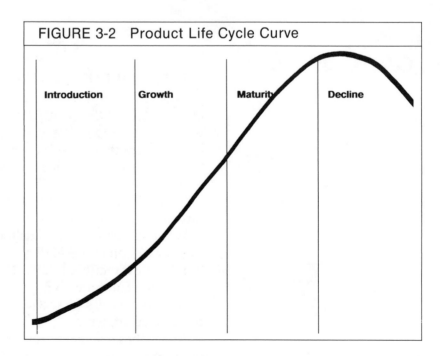

FIGURE 3-2 Product Life Cycle Curve

Introduction   Growth   Maturity   Decline

products? Any organization that is to remain viable must introduce new products to meet the current needs of its customers.

There are four stages in the life cycle of any product or service. Some have a long life cycle while others have a very short one. When we introduce a new service, it will not be adopted by all of our customers at once. Rather, there will be an "adoption curve" that resembles the product life cycle. Where does your library fit on a product life cycle curve?

Place your individual services on a product life cycle curve. Consider services to children, the business community, readers of popular materials, video/audio materials, CD-ROM, and online products.

What have you done to keep traditional services fresh? How have you promoted or changed these services to keep them at the mature part of their life cycle and not let them slip into decline?

Libraries traditionally have a difficult time recognizing that some products/services have reached the declining stage. Some should be discontinued. However, if these products or services seem worthwhile, then perhaps an advertising program can return them to the mature, healthy part of the product life cycle.

4 MARKETING STRATEGIES

So far you have considered goals in association with your objectives, target markets, and position in the marketplace. Now you must develop specific strategies that will provide the roadmap for accomplishing your objectives. Develop specific strategies for each part of the "marketing mix." Determine the attributes of the specific product or service, its price, and a distribution system before you begin to develop promotional plans. Clarify the message before you attempt to take it to the target market.

Since each of these strategies must be carefully considered, market planning takes time. These strategies identify specifically what you will do, who will do it, where you will do it, and how you will promote it. Strategies help us to identify necessary costs, impact on staff, and time required to get the job done.

THE FOUR P'S:

PRODUCT, PRICE, PLACE, AND PROMOTION

The effectiveness of each of your products or services will be determined by the creativity you employ as well as specific targeted efforts you make to implement the marketing strategies. The four P's of marketing are critical elements in effective strategies (Figure 4-1). The best product or service in the world will fail unless these elements are addressed successfully. *Marketing mix* is another term often used to describe the four P's.

We use the marketing planning process not only to develop a new product or service, but also to examine our current services to determine how we can achieve a better performance. We should also use this process to identify which products/services to discontinue.

PRODUCT/SERVICE

The first of your strategies, product, refers to the complete description of the product or service that you are offering. Remember to describe not only the product's attributes, but the benefits of the product to the customer.

Attributes or features refer to specific "bells and whistles." They differentiate your product or service from its competitors. If you were comparing VCR's, for example, you might design a com-

FIGURE 4-1

37

parison chart like the one shown in Figure 4-2. The same chart can be used to list your library's products and services and the benefits they offer your customers. The automated catalog, for example, may contain features or attributes including public access terminals, printers, or remote access through a modem. The benefits to the customer include easy access to up-to-date information from home or office.

As you develop a new service, it is important to remember that it is not the service itself that has value for the customer—it is the benefit of the proposed service that interests the customer (Figure 4-3). For example, if your library has a new automated circulation system, the customer won't care unless it results in some benefit such as greater access to books and other materials or faster check out. Automation is a common goal of libraries.

FIGURE 4-2   Comparison Chart

Product or Service	Features and/or Attributes	Benefits to Customer	How do you provide this service?

FIGURE 4-3 Some New Services and Their Benefits to Customers

Product/Service	Features	Benefit to Customer
Automated Circulation System	• Materials accessible by title, name or word search • Lists of availability of materials	Provides quick and easy access to information
Public Access Terminals	• User friendly terminals located throughout the library	Customer can access information directly
Public Access Copy Machines	• Coin-operated • Collates • Prints two sides	Customer can copy reference materials easily
Children's Summer Reading Program	• Prizes • Special program for children	Children find reading is rewarding and fun
Coin Changing Machines	• Changes $1 bills • Changes $5 bills	Customer has easy access to correct change

However, to develop the necessary support to achieve this goal, you must define the automation by the benefits it brings the customer: automation means that it will be easier to find information about library books and materials and get them.

FEATURES AND BENEFITS

In order to communicate the benefit of a product or service to the customer, you must think like the customer. The customer's point of view becomes the marketing point of view. Look at your library from the outside in. How will your customer benefit from using the services? To be successful, each product or service offered by the library must share six elements of quality. Together these elements produce the benefits that the customer desires:

Performance: For example, fee-based document delivery promises that documents will be delivered in a specified time. Federal Express guarantees its performance with its 24-hour delivery service. Can you provide 24-hour delivery from one location to another in your library?

Features: In a fee-based information delivery service, features would include documents retrieved and level of research performed. This is analogous to the "bells and whistles" of commercial products.

Reliability: High levels of customer satisfaction and high levels of contract renewals indicate that the service is reliable. Never miss a scheduled deadline. If you promise to deliver information or materials within a certain time, be reliable about delivery.

Durability: A product should stand the test of time and consumer usage. Timex watches and Maytag washing machines remind you of the durability of their products. The library buildings provide a sense of the durability of our service.

Esthetics: In the example of a fee-based service, highly qualified professional staff are an esthetic feature; packaging a report in an attractive/pleasant format is an esthetic feature. How are the books and materials displayed in the library? Esthetics refers to a pleasant atmosphere in which your customers can use the service.

Perceived quality: When customers view a service as being of high quality, they will recommend it to other potential customers.

Remember, in a marketing approach it is the customer's perception that counts.

Use the chart in Figure 4-4 to help evaluate your product/service.

PRICE

How is your service priced? Library budgets are typically based on increases to the previous year's budget. As a service industry, the highest costs are in the personnel department. Traditionally, funds for books and materials represent only 10 percent to 20 percent of a library's total budget. As a result, individual programs, services, and products are rarely priced within libraries. However, every service has a price. The cost of books and ma-

---

FIGURE 4-4   Product/Service Evaluation Chart

Service:	Excellent	Very Good	Average	Below Average	Poor
How good is your performance					
How would you rate the features of the service?					
Is this service reliable?					
What about the esthetics in which your provide the service?					
What is the perceived quality of the service?					

terials is only one of the elements in the cost figure. Additional elements include space, personnel, administrative, and other indirect costs.

Determining the actual costs involved in any new product or service is the first step in pricing the service. A decision must be made about whether this service should be "free" or considered a value-added service for which there should be a charge.

Libraries have entered the fee-based arena by charging their customers for the use of copy machines and telefax equipment. In many cases, these charges are based on a review of similar services in the community. Pricing a service by comparing it to similar services in the marketplace is called fair market pricing.

At most libraries, the cost of searching for information using online databases is also passed on to the customer. Prices are usually figured at a cost recovery level—that is, the actual cost of providing the service using online technology is passed on to the customer with no profit to the library.

As you look at costs of providing library services, you will find that several pricing strategies must be considered.

Premium pricing: Consider this for products or services offered at the highest level. Premium pricing strategies are used in pricing luxury automobiles. The level of personal service that accompanies the purchase goes far beyond the actual purchase. In libraries, fee-based research and document delivery might be considered for a premium pricing model. If your service is innovative, in demand, and has little competition, a premium pricing model should be selected. The customer service that you provide to accompany this pricing model must be premium, too.

Competitive pricing: If your service is one of several comparable services in the marketplace, the service should be competitive in price. For example, copy machine and telefax machine use within the library would be competitively priced.

Market penetration (discount pricing): Sometimes manufacturers put a low price on their product to encourage people to buy. This strategy often enables them to make a substantial penetration in the marketplace. Libraries use this method when they provide books and other materials free to the public.

Pricing strategies must be in keeping with your overall financial objectives. Make certain that your pricing strategies are consistent with your overall goals and financial well being. Carefully analyze the actual cost of developing a service. In determining an appro-

FIGURE 4-5   Pricing Strategy Worksheet

Product/Service Costs: $ _____

_____

Staff costs: _____

Facilities costs: _____

Packaging costs: _____

Distribution costs: _____

Promotional costs: _____

Equipment costs: _____

Other costs: _____

TOTAL PRODUCT/SERVICE COSTS: $ _____

Competition: _____   _____

_____   _____

Pricing Strategy: _____   _____

_____   _____

_____   _____

_____   _____

FIGURE 4-6   Worksheet: Place

1. Describe your distribution outlets or locations of your library branches.

_____

_____

_____

2. List changes in population growth or decline that will influence where your library's services will be placed.

_____

_____

_____

3. Will improvements in technology/automation affect the need for physical locations in your system?

_____

_____

_____

4. What other changes in your environment will affect the physical location of your services?

_____

_____

_____

priate pricing structure, identify each component, not only the hard costs, but also the costs of staff time, physical space, administrative overhead, and other costs not easily determined. The worksheet in Figure 4-5 will help you organize your cost analysis.

PLACE

Where will you offer your services? Will they be offered in one location? How have you determined the locations of your service areas? Are there new, creative distribution programs which will make this service more successful?

Place becomes a major issue for library service. Traditionally, place has meant the physical location of branch, academic, and central libraries. Computerized networks, remote access through computer modems, and electronic mail and delivery systems have changed our sense of place to include more than physical access to the library. Can the telephone or online direct access create a greater sense of access to these services?

Manufacturers must consider distribution strategies in a very concrete manner. Should they build additional manufacturing plants to save distribution costs? Retail stores have elaborate plan-

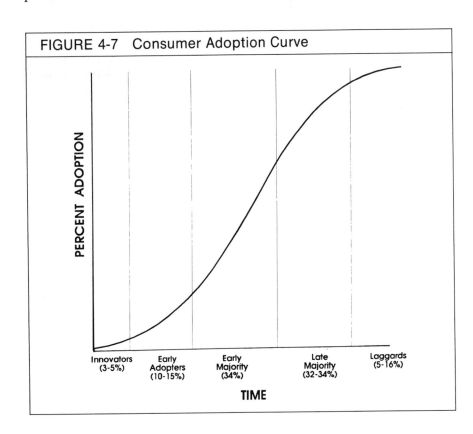

FIGURE 4-7   Consumer Adoption Curve

ning mechanisms to help them decide the most opportune location for their outlets. Place is the key to success for fast food restaurants.

The worksheet in Figure 4-6 will help you analyze the environment in which library marketing plans are developed.

CUSTOMER ADOPTION CURVE

Customers' adoption of new products or services is represented by the curve in Figure 4-7. Every product or service has an adoption curve. Although librarians often expect an immediate reaction by customers to a new product or service, you should be aware that people's normal acceptance of a new product/service is more gradual. The first customers to adopt a new service are called innovators. After the product or service has been available and adopted by a number of customers, additional customers will follow. Promotional efforts will shorten the length of this curve.

POLITICS AND PUBLIC POLICY

Libraries often have to consider an additional two P's in their strategy mix: public policy and politics. Factor them into the li-

FIGURE 4-8 What Political or Public Policy Issues Affect Your Library?	
Political/Public Policy Issues	Possible Solutions

brary's marketing plan. Since budgets are determined through the political process, library programs and services are often limited through political processes. In addition to the usual four P's of marketing, libraries need to develop political strategies. When developing political strategies, careful attention must be paid to individual politicians who are important in the political decision-making process. Apply the first steps in the marketing planning process to identify who they are (segmentation) and what will encourage them to support the library (customer decision-making process).

In many locations, there are public policies that influence the development of programs and services within the library. Public policy includes such items as city ordinances, legal requirements, and legal operating structures. For example, your library may need to comply with a policy that states that money received from customers' payment of library fines goes directly to the city's general fund and cannot be used specifically for library purposes. Marketing planning must take these issues into account. Use the chart in Figure 4-8 to itemize public policy issues that affect your library.

FIGURE 4-9   Some of the Cultural, Social, Political, and Economic Factors that Influence Library Marketing Strategies

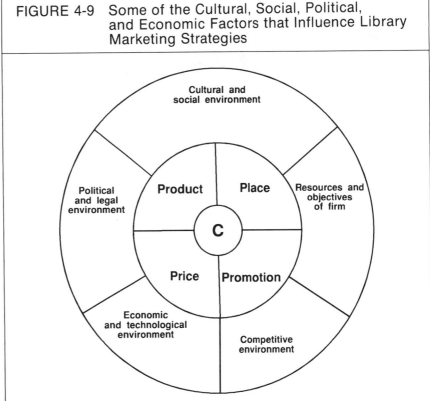

FIGURE 4-10   This Chart Represents the Relationship of Marketing ''Tactics'' to the Marketing Planning Process

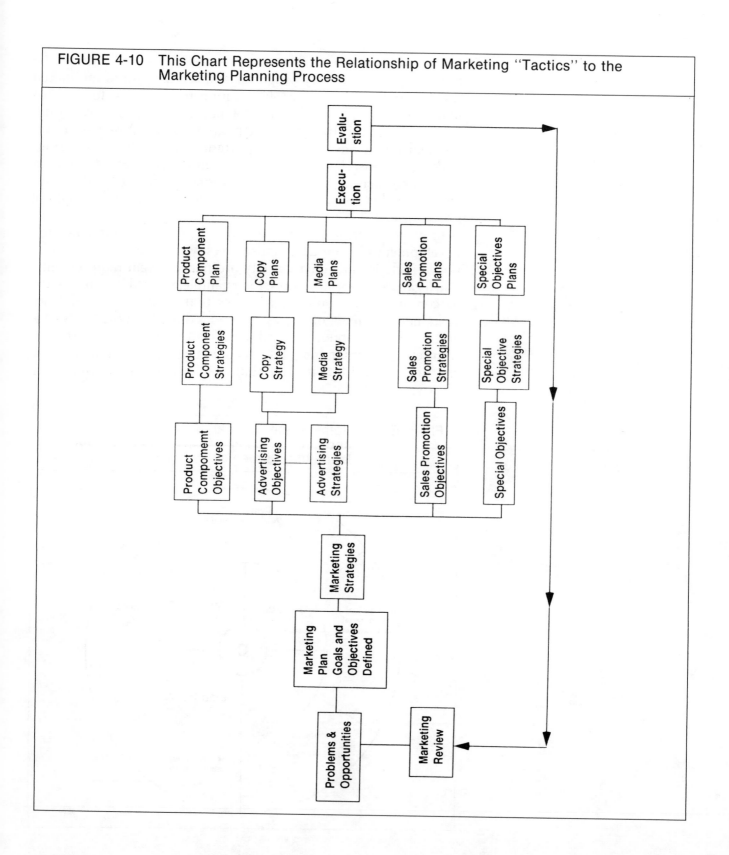

PROMOTIONAL MIX
- Advertising
- Personal selling
- Public relations
- Promotions

PROMOTION

This is one of the largest areas of marketing. It is complex and requires a great deal of creativity as well as planning. Despite the fact that library budgets may not allow for any promotion of their products and services, a promotional effort is key to the success of service marketing. The marketing strategy of promotion includes paid advertising as well as all areas of public relations. It is a broad field. There are many professional firms who specialize in one or two areas of public relations, advertising, and special events. The promotion strategies are very visible, of course. As a result, many individuals believe that the word "marketing" is synonymous with promotion.

Promotion represents *one* of the marketing strategies. A successful marketing plan demands careful attention to each of the strategies.

MARKETING TACTICS

PUBLIC RELATIONS

Public relations can be defined as relationships with all of your publics. Those publics may include the news media, neighborhood associations, present and past customers, politicians, and stakeholders. A library is a business built upon relationships between people.

Positive public relations requires first evaluating public attitudes toward your library. After the evaluation process, it requires planning specific action to create favorable attitudes. Advertising is more controlled because you pay for the space. You cannot control the placement of feature articles in newspapers but you can develop, through research and planning, consistent and targeted communications that will result in positive media coverage. Public relations programs require time and expertise.

SOME PR TOOLS FOR LIBRARIES

Research, planning, and evaluation: Research and know the appropriate editors, publishers, and reporters of newspapers in your area, as well as people in television, including cable television, and radio. You can get specific information through local press associations. In smaller communities, you can call neighborhood publications, radio stations, and newspapers. They will usually be quite responsive and give you the name of the appropriate individuals.

Press relations: Understand how your local press operates. Is there competition between publications? Identify key individuals with whom you should work. Call and make an appointment to get acquainted. Use your library network to identify appropriate contacts. Library Board members and Friends can be a source of information.

News and feature writing: Will your local newspaper work with you to develop a feature article? What is news in their eyes? You can get some information based on reading their papers.

Seminars and workshops: Seminars and workshops on topics like "How to Do a Patent Search," "How to Get a Job," "Financial Planning," or "How to Publish a Book," can be public relations tools for libraries.

Speeches: Speeches on subjects relevant to specific organizations can create positive public relations for libraries. Community organizations and civic clubs are always in need of programs and welcome speakers who are well prepared.

Special events: Ground breakings, ribbon cuttings, celebrities reading stories to children, an author reading from his or her book, and booksales are all examples of special events that create good public relations. Take time to make some of your events special by inviting a local politician to participate. Create "good news" events out of market research reports.

Special features: Various radio stations, *Sesame Street*, and some fast-food restaurants have created giant animal or bird mascots to attract attention. The Denver Public Library has a "book worm" that appears at children's events in various centers. It has received front-page, color coverage in a local newspaper. The Denver Public Library's "Now Famous Book Clappers and Kazoo Band" has won many local awards for its marching. The library has received recognition by the appearance of the band in parades covered by television and press. Volunteer employees who are drilled in their routines by a fellow staffer make up the band.

THE LIBRARY'S PUBLICS INCLUDE:

Employees:

- Managers
- Clerical staff
- New employees
- Employee families
- Professional staff
- Retired employees
- Outstanding employees

The library's funders—public sources:

- City council
- Mayor
- City budget office
- Angry politicians
- Campaigning politicians

- City manager
- Elected officials
- State legislators
- Politicians with a "stake"
- The electorate

The library's funders—private sources:

- Corporations
- Foundations
- Individuals

The media:

- General press
- Business press
- Library press
- Wire services
- Local weekly publications
- Business newsletters
- Electronic media
- Friendly journalists
- Hostile journalists
- Outstanding journalists
- Community publications

Library customers:

- Satisfied
- Dissatisfied
- New
- Old
- Potential
- Special segments
  —Children
  —Minorities
  —Elderly
  —Special Interest Groups
  —Neighborhoods
  —Students
  —Educators
  —Community Groups

List your publics:

_____

_____

_____

_____

_____

WORKING WITH THE NEWS MEDIA

Obtaining the support of the news media is very important. Feature articles in newspapers and magazines bring a great deal of credibility to the service you provide. In fact, there is no way you could gain such credibility through advertising. Steps to take in reaching the media include:

Research: Identify the editors and specialists in the media. Get to know them and the kind of articles they want. Know their publication dates, how copy should be prepared, and with whom to work. The best way to research is to get on the phone personally and ask for information.

Write copy in an easy-to-read format: Submit it and follow up. Many times a paper will not use the copy as submitted, or will delay printing until a later edition. Send it to the appropriate individual. If you don't, it may not be printed. Follow up with a telephone call. Use short sentences and keep your articles brief.

Research television as well: Introduce yourself to key individuals. Persistence and networking pay off. Some television stations have a public affairs director who determines the station's involvement with the library. This person is called a "gatekeeper" because he or she can determine the level of support for your program. Spend time with these individuals in advance of any specific request.

WRITING A PRESS RELEASE

- Write it on library letterhead or special library press-release letterhead that identifies your library

- Identify the contact person in the library (usually the person writing the release)
- Date the release
- Start with a headline
- Always double space the text
- Keep it simple
- Give accurate facts

WAYS TO MAKE NEWS

Libraries must seek ways to make news. Think of "good news" events that will attract coverage. The tactics listed below will create positive awareness among your selected target audiences:

- *Tie in with the news events of the day.* Provide news media with contacts in the library who can verify information.
- *Tie in with other publicity events.* For example, National Library Week.
- *Tie in with media on a mutual project.* Television, newspapers, and radio stations sponsor a few events. They provide substantial publicity for the events they choose to sponsor.
- *Conduct a poll or survey and release results.* If you do market research studies, publish the results.
- *Issue a report.* When your circulation has increased, write a report and send it to the local press.
- *Arrange an interview with a celebrity.* Ask sports figures and other celebrities to participate in children's story hours or other events.
- *Arrange a testimonial.*
- *Celebrate an anniversary.* Involve the community. Ask a local bakery to bake a large cake. Invite the mayor and other elected officials to the party. Ask local entertainers to perform.
- *Tie in with a holiday.* Host a Christmas party or a Halloween party for kids or seniors. Again, ask local bakeries to provide refreshments and a local bank or retail store to provide invitations.
- *Stage a debate.*
- *Appear on radio or TV talk shows.*
- *Write a monthly book review in the local paper.* Develop lists of new books that have just arrived in the library for your column.
- *Photographs.* A photo of the mayor reading stories to children almost always gets printed in local newspapers.

- *Slide shows.* Well-prepared slide shows are popular as programs for neighborhood groups and social groups.
- *Host a local contest or tournament.* Want to reach young adults? Host a contest or tournament with a popular game. Ask the producer of the game to provide copies at no charge. Ask a local bank to sponsor the game by providing prize money and printing. Promote the game/tournament through local schools. Everyone wins in this kind of program. The bank looks like a good citizen. The game producer gets publicity. And the library appeals to young adults.
- *Host a contest for senior citizens.* Seniors love bingo, of course. They love events and tournaments that challenge their minds. Again, a local company can work with you as a sponsor.

ADVERTISING

Advertising is different from public relations. It is any paid form of presentation or promotion of ideas, goods, or services by an identified sponsor. When we pay for it, we control the message, the time it is given, and the delivery method.

STEPS IN CREATING ADVERTISING

1. *First identify one program or service you want to promote.* Then develop your "unique selling proposition." This is a statement that makes a person want to use your service. It can be the same as your positioning statement.
2. *Develop a creative plan with details of both your public relations and advertising program.* This plan will also identify your mix of creative products, including direct mail, signs, telephone book advertisements, open houses, news events, and newspaper and radio ads. Place a budget around this program. Identify staff time required and decide which one of these programs is the most important to you.
3. *Develop quantitative objectives.* How many people will be drawn to your program or service by each form of advertising or public relations? Market penetration, ticket sales, number of people in attendance, circulation mea-

surements, and increased card registration are examples of easily quantifiable objectives. At first, you will have to make a reasonable guess. As you gain experience with this kind of estimation and track your customers, you will find which promotion or advertising is most effective.

4. *Establish specific goals and objectives so you have targets for which to aim.* Having specific goals and objectives forces you to use data effectively and establish priorities for activities. It also gives you an idea of the resources needed to attain them and forces you to realize that some of your goals are unrealistic and should be eliminated.

5. *Don't spread yourself too thin.* When mistakes occur, it is usually because we have not provided sufficient time to do a good job of promotion. We mail invitations too late and don't take the time for the personal contact that is the key to success. Budget time and effort to the promotional methods that will work most successfully, and do it well.

Credibility: If people don't believe your advertising, they won't try the service.

Longevity: Determine advertising strategies and keep the campaign in front of the target audience long enough to establish recognition.

Continuity: Develop a plan and stick to it. Concentrate on a few areas of greatest effectiveness and put enough money into it to generate recognition.

DO IT YOURSELF

Recent changes in technology allow us the opportunity to create our own advertising. Through personal computers, desktop publishing software, and scanners you can create ads for print media as well as brochures, posters, and bookmarks.

- Gather all the facts—date, time, location, ticket price. Ask yourself who, what, when, where.
- Remember your unique selling point. Capture your message in a simple phrase.
- Don't try to tell the whole story in a single ad. When you design your first ad, go back and take out half the copy.
- Put yourself in the place of the prospective client.
- Remember the KISS rule: Keep it simple, stupid.

SELECTING AN AGENCY

Advertising agencies occasionally "adopt" a nonprofit organization. They will develop a full advertising campaign and call on other vendors to provide material, shoot commercials, and donate their services. They will work with the media to get placement of print and media advertisement. Advertising federations or clubs also have public service committees that will work with nonprofit organizations on a campaign.

Advertising agencies are in the business of producing the programs to sell your service. You must be very clear on the selling points of your service before you begin to work with an agency to develop the advertisement.

- Develop your marketing goals and objectives.
- Identify your target audiences.
- Define parameters (dates) of campaign.
- Identify resources to support campaign.
- Identify prospective advertising agencies, large and small.
- Study campaigns they have done for other clients.
- Seek client recommendations.
- Choose an agency that works well with you.

WORKING WITH AN AGENCY

Here are some general guidelines to keep in mind:

- Select *one* individual who will work with the agency. It is very confusing for an ad agency to work with a group of volunteers.
- Give your representative clear directions. Identify the scope of the program or service you want to promote.
- Define your specific target audiences. Don't try to reach everyone with one campaign.
- Develop marketing goals and objectives and specific advertising objectives.
- Be sure that the appropriate people have an opportunity to participate in and approve of the objectives of the campaign before giving creative direction to the campaign. Make sure your group agrees on the direction, target audience, and objectives. Then *trust* the agency.
- Develop time lines.
- Agree on financial estimates before work is begun.
- The advertising agency will develop a story board or outline before developing a full campaign. If desirable, this story board can be tested in a focus group setting to determine effectiveness of communication strategy.

- Remember that the ad agency knows the advertising business better than you do.
- Present the ad campaign to staff, Trustees, and Friends before it appears on television, radio, or in print. Introduce the campaign in a spirit of celebration, perhaps including buttons, t-shirts, or other items.
- Develop a point-of-sale campaign to reinforce the campaign in the agency. Examples of point-of-sale items are posters and buttons.

CHOOSING MEDIA

Newspapers: Call your local newspaper about the opportunity to use small "drop-in" ads that appear every time the paper has space. Prepare ads in specific sizes and provide copies to the newspapers. These ads can feature specific programs or services and will be printed at no charge to you.

Television: Television stations do provide time for nonprofit organizations. However, free time usually means that ads do not appear at prime time. At some television and cable stations, public affairs department personnel will assist you in developing advertising. In addition, some of these stations sponsor events and programs, which they promote heavily.

Radio: Radio stations clearly identify their target market. If you want to consider radio advertising, ask local stations to provide you with information on their listeners. Prime advertising time on radio is "drive time." You should select radio stations whose target audience matches the segment that you are trying to reach. Many stations broadcast a community calendar that will list your program or event at no cost.

Phone book: Don't forget the yellow pages of your local phone book. Short advertisements should be placed in many different areas of the directory.

TV: STRENGTHS AND LIMITATIONS

Advantages include:

- TV offers opportunities to reach the largest audience with one advertising message. Over 95 percent of American homes have television sets.

- The cost per exposure is not too high if your message is brief and is aired on cable TV or during a non-prime-time hour.
- TV utilizes many elements: sight, sound, motion, color, and demonstration.
- Each message is seen full screen, center stage.
- Audience selectivity is possible.
- Cable television is bringing another concept and availability to TV advertising.

Disadvantages include:

- Cost can be prohibitive if you are aiming for a network channel during peak evening viewing hours.
- TV ads need repetition to be effective.
- Prime time is evening only; public service spots are often shown after midnight.
- "Creativity" for its own sake can make viewers forget the message.
- Cable, video, and remote control devices have altered the reach of television advertising—the number of people who see the commercial. Television audiences tend to be quite large and may be too diffuse to capture your target audience well.

If you can produce your own television spot, public service announcements are reasonable. Few television stations will produce them for you.

RADIO: STRENGTHS AND LIMITATIONS

Advantages include:

- Greatest opportunity for immediacy.
- Can reach almost all Americans.
- Offers great selectivity.
- Adaptable, can change easily.
- Adults spend more time with radio than any other medium except TV.
- Radio is particularly useful for special events and programs.

Disadvantages include:

- Radio has lost some of its prestige.
- The lack of a visual image limits its communication capabilities.
- Since radio listening is often shared with another activity, audience attention is shared. People listen while driving, working, cleaning house.
- The radio message is fleeting and perishable.
- The large number of radio stations in a locality creates an audience that is fragmented.
- You must pick both station and time of day carefully in order to be effective.

DIRECT MAIL

Electronic circulation systems offer libraries opportunities to use their customer database to provide direct mail service by segments. Direct-mail solicitation is used frequently to develop a membership program. Again, segmentation is of the utmost importance. Research by the Denver Public Library Friends group indicated that women over the age of 55 were most responsive to a direct-mail solicitation to become members. This segment was then targeted for a direct-mail campaign.

Since a "normal" response rate is one percent, this type of promotional activity can seem quite expensive. The key to success is repetition. Consider mailing up to three times per year to increase your response rate.

There are many variables to be considered when developing a direct mail appeal or promotion. They include:

- *Timing.* When will your mailing arrive?
- *Packaging.* What does the mailing look like? Subtleties like the choice of a postage stamp and the color and shape of the piece will affect the response rate.
- *Letter or appeal.* People read the postscript and special quotes first.
- *Ease of response.* Have you enclosed an envelope for quick response? Do you provide postage?
- *Get through the clutter.* Be creative in your appeal. How will your piece of direct mail stand out?

Direct mail can be very effective with some target audiences. Children who participated in a focus group study at Denver Public Library indicated that they wanted to receive mail addressed to them at home. They explained that their parents received volumes of mail, but they rarely received anything addressed to them.

TELEMARKETING

A direct mail appeal combined with a telemarketing effort will increase the response rate. Telemarketing is a disciplined, planned effort to reach customers through the use of the telephone. Telemarketing is very helpful in renewing Friends memberships, enlisting volunteers, and building audiences.

Libraries tend to shy away from telemarketing. None of us likes to be called by sales people at dinner time. However, phone calls coming from library staff and volunteers are usually well received. They are the only time that library customers hear directly and personally from the library. The phone calls asking for support of a membership program or special event will provide a unique opportunity to learn how the library is perceived by your customers.

A training session should be held for volunteers. Your success depends heavily on both a pre-developed script and the individuals who do the phoning. Make the training and actual telemarketing sessions fun. Provide food and drink.

Ask a local real estate company or bank to donate their offices and phone system to be used in a telemarketing campaign.

The personal telephone call from a library volunteer can be most effective in renewing memberships, acquiring private donations, and developing voter support.

NOW, THE ACTION PLAN

Use the worksheets in Figures 5-1 and 5-2 to determine your strategies for success and to position your library's products and services. Next, identify tactics. A specific schedule of activities that will assist you in meeting each of your strategies is shown in Figures 5-3 and 5-4. You should identify the individual responsible for each tactic, the budget required, and the length of time required for the activity. All of this can fit on a flow chart (Figure 5-5). It is helpful to place the required tactics on a large calendar on the wall. To think of each strategy, you must think of each activity in detail. List the activities in order and assign an individual to be responsible.

FIGURE 5-1   Marketing Strategies Worksheet

(Example)

Goal #1: Service Goal

Target market #1:

OBJECTIVES: (Should relate to this segment of the target market.)
1.
2.
3.

STRATEGIES (The Marketing Mix)

1. List product or service strategies, particular customer benefits and/or attributes.

2. List place/distribution strategies.

3. List price strategies. (Include funding source.)

4. Promotion strategies
   a. Public relations

   b. Promotion/events

   c. Advertising

   d. Direct mail

   e. Other

5. Internal considerations
   a. How much staff time will strategies require?

   b. How much volunteer or support group time will strategies require?

   c. How much will strategies cost?

Repeat the same steps for each target market of each goal. Then assemble the information to evaluate appropriateness.

FIGURE 5-2   Appropriateness of Strategy

Strategy	Appropriate /Realistic?	Do they reach target?	Will desired result be reached?	Priority of strategy?	Are staff strengths/ weaknesses recognized?
PRICE					
PROMO-TION					
PRODUCT					
PLACE					

FIGURE 5-3   Marketing Tactics

Strategy:	Development of new Product or Service	Place - How distribution channels to be set up?	Promotion - P/R, advertising	Price - Public funds, private funds, fee based services
WHO				
WHAT				
WHERE				
WHEN				
HOW MUCH				

FIGURE 5-4   Marketing Tactics

Tactic	Budget	Time Needed	Responsibility	Specific Step
Advertising:				
Newspapers:				
Other Publications				
Radio				
Direct Mail				
Public Relations:				
Interviews				
Feature Stories				
Special appearances				
Events				

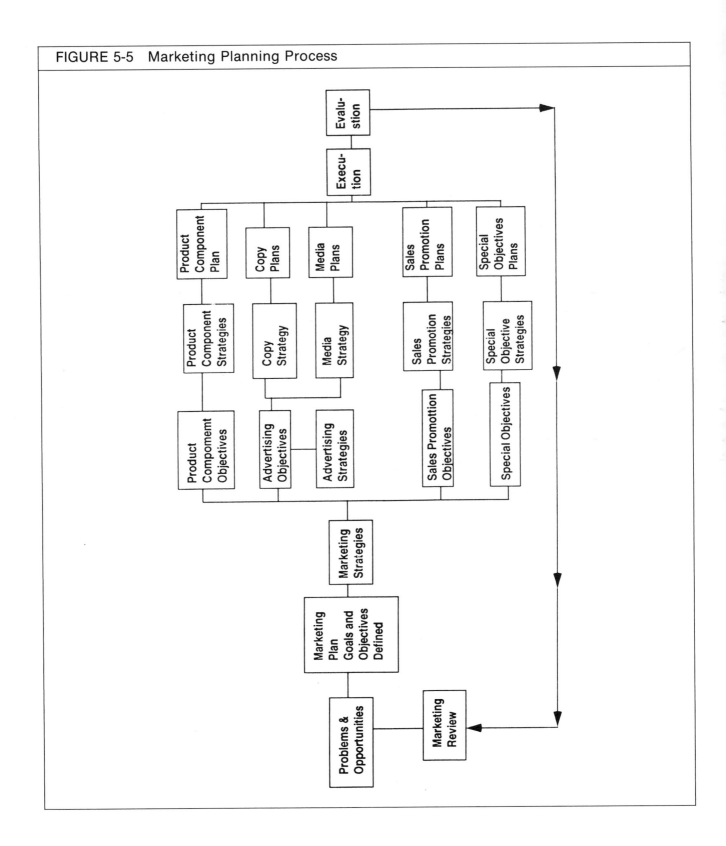

FIGURE 5-5 Marketing Planning Process

6 EVALUATION

A marketing approach to services provides the necessary analysis and planning that will guarantee success. However, a mistake may result from the failure to carry out an individual step of the process. It is important that we look at our work and evaluate the process. We may be able to correct a mistake in the product strategy or in promotional efforts, correct the problem, and create a successful product or service in the future. It is very easy to say, "It didn't work," when really the issue was not paying specific attention to a crucial detail.

When something goes wrong, ask yourself:

- Is there an error in the plan?
- Were the original objectives valid?
- Did you analyze each of the strategies?
- Was there sufficient time allowed for the action steps?
- What corrective steps are to be taken?

You should evaluate your efforts after each program or service has been introduced. Often it is beneficial to do it with a group of people who were involved with the introduction process. Talk about your successes. Where did things really go well? Talk about the mistakes that were made and steps that could have been improved.

Mistakes can occur because we underestimate the time required to promote the services. It is better to reduce the number of strategies and tactics. Implement fewer individual tactics, but do them really well. The overall results will be better.

WORKSHEET

MARKETING PLAN EVALUATION PROCESS

Identify your goal:

_____

_____

Objectives:

_____

_____

_____

_____

Was your goal achieved? _____

What were the actual results of your objectives?

_____

_____

_____

_____

Environmental analysis:

1. Were the original assumptions correct?

   _____

   _____

2. What additional assumptions should be considered?

   _____

   _____

3. Did you assess your strengths and weaknesses accurately?

   _____

   _____

4. What additional strengths or weaknesses affect the success of the program?

_____

_____

5. Did you correctly identify the appropriate segment for this program?

_____

_____

6. Were you accurate in your estimation of demand?

_____

_____

7. Did your competitive analysis provide you with correct information?

_____

_____

8. What did you identify as the key element in the customer decision-making process? Was that element correct?

_____

_____

THE "MARKETING MIX" OR MARKETING STRATEGIES

Product/Service:

1. Describe the product or service including "features" and "benefits." Do you feel that the product or service had the appropriate "features" and "benefits"?

_____

_____

2. How could the product be improved?

_____

_____

Price:

1. Describe your pricing (or funding) strategy

_____

_____

2. Was the price too high? too low? funding inadequate?

_____

_____

3. Were the costs underestimated? overestimated?

_____

_____

4. Recommended changes for pricing strategy

_____

_____

Place/Distribution:

1. Identify your place or distribution strategy

_____

_____

2. What were the issues with this strategy?

_____

_____

3. What changes need to be made in this strategy?

_____

_____

Promotion:

1. Identify the promotion strategies

_____

_____

_____

2. What was your response to each strategy? In other words, how many individuals responded to newspaper advertisements? To direct mail?

_____

_____

_____

3. What changes would you make in the area of promotion strategies?

_____

_____

_____

Marketing tactics:

1. Identify specific tactics
   Advertising
   Direct Mail
   Press Relations
   Sales
   Other

2. Which of the tactics was most successful?

_____

_____

_____

3. Did you allow enough time to carry out the tactics? If no, which ones required more time than you thought?

_____

_____

_____

4. What changes in tactics would you recommend for the future?

_____

_____

_____

Budget:

1. What was the actual budget for the project?

_____

_____

_____

2. What were the actual costs?

_____

_____

_____

3. What were the actual revenues?

_____

_____

_____

_____

SUMMARY

What changes in the marketing plan would lead to a more successful project?

_____

_____

_____

_____

7 A SAMPLE MARKETING PLAN

The staff of the XYZ Public Library want to establish an annual program that will position the library in the community as a cultural center. They want to use a marketing planning process to design and implement an annual poetry series featuring nationally recognized poets within the library.

ENVIRONMENTAL ANALYSIS

Strengths of the library and its staff:

1. Central location of the library
2. Enthusiasm and knowledge of the staff

Weaknesses of library:

1. Lack of staff time for adequate planning
2. Lack of a budget to support such a program
3. Minimal staff skills in areas of promotion.

General assumptions that could affect success of program:

1. There is a strong private and public education system within the community that would support such a program.
2. The demographics and lifestyle information regarding the community indicates that there would be a strong interest by the community.

SEGMENTATION

How would you begin to define the segment or segments of individuals who would like the opportunity to hear poets reading and discussing their work? While they have a common affection for poetry, they are probably quite different in other characteristics. Poetry enthusiasts may enjoy the poetry of a specific poet, era, nationality, or ethnic group. They may be further segmented by age, location of residence, or economic factors. Therefore, the general poetry lover audience probably consists of several segments. These individual segments are defined by the kind of poetry that they like.

English teachers are a second segment. However, they also include subsegments and can be further divided by specific grade, achievement level, or specific school. They can be segmented by those who teach at public schools and those who teach at private schools.

Students can also be further defined in our segmentation analysis by grade, achievement level, and type of school they attend.

DEMAND

The potential demand from each of these segments needs to be evaluated. When a marketing plan is developed, consider the factors that will affect the demand for the product or service. In the case of this proposed poetry series, factors that affect the demand for each segment include:

Segment	Factors affecting demand
Individuals who like poetry	Time of presentation, location, day of week, availability of parking, price of tickets, effectiveness of promotion, poets selected.
Teachers	Poets selected, price, day and time, effective, personalized promotion to reach these individuals.
Students	Is attendance required as a part of their English class? Can they obtain extra credit for attending? Is a group discount available? Will the school provide transportation?

As we begin to estimate the potential demand for the service, we identify how many individuals there are in each segment. As we begin to understand the actual numbers of individuals in each segment who might want to attend a poetry series, we can decide which segment of the market will become our niche market for this particular product or service.

CUSTOMER DECISION-MAKING PROCESS

In this case, the factors affecting demand provide a guide to the decision-making process of the customer. This process, of course, varies with the segment of the customer base under consideration.

The decision-making process of customers who enjoy poets and poetry reading probably depends on such variables as: the specific poets selected, the availability of parking, the convenience of time, and the promotion and pricing strategies.

For teachers the decision-making process might also involve the appropriateness of the poets for classroom application as well as the pricing and transportation package.

There will be strong student attendance if the series is required or if extra credit is offered. Price and transportation will also play an important role.

COMPETITION

Although there will probably not be any other poetry series offered at the same time, competition for all of the segments identified will come from other school and social activities, television programs, and other cultural events. Even Monday night football on television could be considered as competition. Careful selection of day of week, time, and location will serve to minimize competition.

WRITING THE PLAN

Goal: The XYZ Library will develop and produce an annual Poetry Series featuring nationally recognized poets reading and discussing their works.

WRITING THE PLAN

OBJECTIVES

1. To have an average audience size of 300 people
2. To generate press and media coverage
3. To raise $1,000 from local business in sponsorship
4. To receive a grant from the local arts council in the amount of $2,500
5. To obtain the participation of one Pulitzer Prize winning poet

TARGET MARKET #1: FRIENDS OF THE LIBRARY

Objective: To sell 10 patron tickets to Friends
Objective: To sell 20 series tickets to Friends
Objective: To encourage 20 Friends to volunteer to assist the project

Segment: Friends of the Library

Demand: The XYZ Library has 500 members of its Friends group.

Competition: Family activities, television specials, and other social activities.

Customer decision-making process: Members of the Friends will participate if:

1. They are involved in the planning process or
2. If they are invited by a friend, or
3. If the group is volunteering to coordinate the reception.

The marketing mix

Product strategies: One Pulitzer Prize winning poet will be selected as a primary attraction. Other poets who are well known will be selected.

Place strategy: A central location will be selected. It should have adequate and safe parking, good ambiance, good acoustics, and adequate facilities for a reception.

Time: The program will be offered on Tuesday evening to avoid local symphony performances, Monday night football, and other cultural and school events.

Pricing strategy: Friends will be offered a special opportunity to be a Patron Sponsor of the event. Patrons will have reserved seating for the events. They will be invited to a private reception/dinner party to meet the poets. Patron tickets will include a tax deductible donation. Other Friends will be offered a discount on series tickets as a "benefit" for being a member of the organization. Individuals can joint the Friends and receive the discount for the series.

Promotion: A special invitation will be sent to the Friends at their homes. A member of the Friends will be on the planning committee. That member will identify and invite individuals to become patrons of the series. This individual will also develop a volunteer committee to work at receptions, transportation, and greeting for the poets. The Friends of the Library will be listed as a major sponsor of the event.

Internal considerations: Amount of time these strategies will require. A great deal of time is often required to identify volunteer leadership and participation. Encouraging the sale of patron tickets is often best done on an individual basis. Volunteer leadership is the key to participation of the group.

TARGET MARKET #2: POETRY ENTHUSIASTS

Objectives:

1. To sell 100 series tickets to this group
2. To promote the series in five local bookstores
3. To promote the series in local coffee houses

Segment: General adult poetry enthusiasts

Demand: It is difficult to estimate the demand by general adult poetry enthusiasts. One could estimate that based on sales of poetry by bookstores or by circulation within the library.

Customer decision-making process: The customers will base their decision on the poets included in the series, the price, the time, and location of the readings. The primary challenge in influencing their decision-making process is reaching them with the appropriate information.

Competition: Monday night football, family activities, other cultural and social events.

The marketing mix

Product and place: Will have the same attributes as the Friends.

Price: A discount for the series will encourage poetry enthusiasts to buy a ticket for the full series even though they may only recognize one poet.

Promotion: Reaching a broad audience on a limited budget can be difficult. Posters will be distributed in local bookstores and coffee houses. Efforts will be made to gain exposure in local newspapers as well as in special arts publications.

Public service announcements: PSAs will be produced for local radio stations including public broadcast radio station and classical music station. These two stations will be asked to "sponsor" the event through publicity.

Community calendars: A general campaign will be developed to create community wide awareness of the poetry series.

Posters/bookmarks: These items will be distributed to local bookstores, coffee houses.

Sales promotions: Ticket outlets will be established at local bookstores.

Internal considerations: The time required to get a feature article in the local press can be significant. Time is also required to develop a good working relationship with local bookstores in order to promote this series.

TARGET MARKET #3: ENGLISH TEACHERS AND HIGH SCHOOL STUDENTS

Objectives:

1. To reach all of the identified English teachers personally.
2. To have four English teachers bring their classes to the poetry sessions.
3. To sell an average of 60 tickets per poet's performance to this target market.

The marketing mix

Product: Poets selected should be appropriate and endorsed by English teachers.

Price: Group pricing should be available at reduced rates to allow teachers the opportunity to bring their class to the sessions. In some private schools, funds are available for such an outing.

In others, individual students would be required to purchase tickets.

Place: Many private schools provide bus or van transportation to these events. Transportation or the availability of parking will be an important element.

Promotion:

- *A personalized appeal.* This target audience will require a very personalized promotion appeal. Each English teacher should be identified and receive a personal letter about the poetry series. Group ticket pricing should be explained. Follow-up telephone calls made by volunteers will strengthen the program.
- *Posters and brochures.* These items should be distributed to schools and classrooms where possible.

Internal considerations:

- *Amount of time strategies will require.* In this case, a volunteer who is a locally recognized teacher will provide better access to other teachers.
- *Cost of strategies.* Actual costs for printed materials is very low. However, personalized letters require the expense of clerical assistance.
- *Staff required by strategies.* While volunteers can work with teachers, staff time will be required in developing an accurate list and in implementing personalized correspondence.

TARGET MARKET #4: FANS OF EACH POET

If one of the poets were of a particular ethnic background, such as African American, a new target audience would be identified. Each poet in the series may attract a particular audience segment.

Objectives:

1. To sell 100 tickets to this particular event.
2. To identify service organizations that will sponsor a reception and host this poet.

A marketing mix of strategies is needed to achieve these objectives:

Product: A well-known African American poet will be included in the series, thus influencing another target market to attend at least one of the offerings.

Place: Centralized location remains important.

Price: Group pricing will be available for social organizations, sororities, fraternal organizations, schools.

Promotion: PSAs will be provided for radio stations whose primary audience is African American.

Posters: Series posters will be provided to bookstores and coffee houses in African American neighborhoods. Individual flyers concerning the poet will be produced and distributed.

Networking: Personal involvement of leaders in the African American community will be the key to success. Often this requires one-on-one meetings with appropriate individuals. Project enough lead time to involve the whole community in the opportunity.

Presentation to organizations: A volunteer will make a personalized appeal to specific African American organizations to sponsor the poet, provide a reception, or to host the poet's visit.

Direct mail: Sending notices to public and private school English teachers, especially to African American teachers, will encourage attendance.

Promotion: A special appearance by the poet in a classroom setting during the day will increase good will in the community. Press coverage can be encouraged.

Internal considerations:

- *Time invested in implementing strategies.* These particular strategies are time-consuming. Volunteer commitment will assist in meeting these requirements.

- *Costs of strategies.* Strategies are highly personalized and, therefore, costly if professional staff time is required.
- *Staffing needed.* Staff supervision and involvement is important to oversee volunteer efforts.

THE ACTION PLAN

The first step is to think through each strategy. At the end of this chapter are worksheets and charts to help you map your plan. What are the activities required to make each strategy work? How much will each strategy cost? Remember, for example, that producing a brochure is a strategy. That strategy requires many different action steps. You must identify who, what, when, and where, as well as how much. Then you must work with a graphic designer to develop copy. The design must be approved, proofed, and printed. You must decide on a mailing process and procure mailing labels.

BUDGET

A budget should be developed to clearly identify accurate costs for the program. Careful examination of the steps in each strategy will provide accurate budget information. A sample budget form is given in the following section of worksheets and examples.

STAYING ON SCHEDULE

The most common error in the marketing plan is developing an unrealistic schedule. Specific steps that have been identified to create a successful program often are ignored altogether or compressed until they lose their effectiveness. Usually these efforts occur in the promotion strategy area. As a result, the attendance at the specific program is lower than desired. The result may be demoralizing to both staff and volunteers.

IDENTIFYING PROBLEM AREAS

Work with staff and volunteers to identify specific problem areas. Compare your actual plan with the originally designed one. Identify specific budget areas, as well as areas of incomplete timing. Review original objectives. Were they reasonable? Were the specific strategies reasonable? What unexpected elements affected your marketing plan?

RECOMMENDATIONS FOR THE FUTURE
Put recommended changes in writing. Identify specific problem areas as well as corrective measures. Use the Evaluation Worksheet at the end of this chapter to assess the program as a whole.

FIGURE 7-1   Strategy Summary Worksheet

Service Strategies	**Will this strategy maximize attendance?**
Attract one Pulitzer Prize-winning poet.	Pulitzer is a national award of significance and so will encourage attendance.
Attract one poet highly recommended by bookstore owners/managers and English teachers.	Support from local English teachers and bookstores will encourage success.
Attract one African American poet.	This will be successful if appropriate promotional strategies are used.

FIGURE 7-2   Pricing Strategies

Pricing Strategies	Does the pricing strategy mix allow for a successful cost recovery program?
Apply for grant from the local arts council to support program.	
Seek sponsorship for receptions.	
Develop group discount pricing strategy for school classes.	
Provide series tickets at discount to encourage attendance.	
Establish discount series tickets for Friends of the Library and senior citizens.	
Set ticket price for an individual event at cost recovery basis.	

FIGURE 7-3 Place Strategies

Place Strategies	Will this strategy encourage attendance?
A church is selected in a central location.	
Parking is available.	
Is the location handicapped-accessible?	

FIGURE 7-4   Promotion Strategies

Promotion Strategies	Does the strategy reach the potential customer most effectively?
Posters, brochures, bookmarks distributed to bookstores, libraries, coffee houses.	
Personalized letter campaign to English teachers at private and public schools.	
Personalized contact with ethnic service clubs to sponsor African American poet.	
Scheduled interviews with local press and other media.	
PSA s to all local media; listing in all local events calendars.	
Development of volunteer committee to encourage ticket sales locally.	
Personalized invitation to Friends of the Library.	

FIGURE 7-5   Strategy Work Sheet

Strategy: Select three poets, including one Pulitzer Prize winning poet and one African American poet.

Start date: _____   Completion date: _____

Activity:

1. Form a voluntary committee that includes a member from the Friends, a librarian, a program coordinator, and a bookstore professional.

2. Develop criteria for selection of poets.

3. Identify budget "boundaries."

4. Identify potential poets for consideration.

5. Identify availability of poets and fee structure.

6. Communicate with specific poets and establish contractual agreement.

FIGURE 7-6 Strategy: Development of Brochure and Poster

Action Step	Description	Date	Who	Cost
Coordinate all tasks.	Who, What, Where, When, Pricing Options	15 hours	Coordinator	
Review design and layout.				
Proofread "blue line" of brochure & poster.				
Authorized printing of both.				
Procure mailing labels.				

FIGURE 7-7   Strategies in Our Poet Series Requiring Specific Action Steps

1.   Development of volunteer committee to select poets and to stimulate ticket sales.

2.   Selection of appropriate poets.

3.   Development of poster and brochure.

4.   Selection of facility for event.

5.   Promotion with ethnic service organizations.

6.   Grant application process for arts council funding.

7.   Personalized promotion process to English teachers in private and public schools.

8.   PSA's for print and electronic and media.

9.   Calendar listings in print and electronic media.

10.   Development of volunteer group to act as hosts for poets, ushers, reception attendants, and ticket takers.

11.   Press relations for specific press article and coverage.

12.   Establishment of ticket sales outlets.

13.   Development of accounting and sales procedures for ticket sales.

14.   Procedure for handling ticket sales within library.

15.   Direct mail to Friends of the Library.

FIGURE 7-8   Action Plan

Specific Action Steps	Who	Start Date	Completion
1.			
2.			
3.			
4.			
5.			
6.			
7.			
8.			
9.			
10.			
11.			
12.			
13.			
14.			
15.			

FIGURE 7-9 Budget

Revenues:

Grant from local arts council	$2,500
Sponsorship of receptions	900
Corporate sponsorship	1,000

Ticket sales

Patron tickets (10 × $100)	1,000
Series tickets (100 × $40)	4,000
Students tickets (75 × $30)	2,250
Friends/Seniors (40 × $30)	1,200
Individual	
(60 × 2 × $15)	1,800
(100 × $15)	1,500
Total revenues:	$16,150

Ticket prices:

- Individual, $15

- Series, $40

- Student Series, $30

- Senior/Friends Series, $30

FIGURE 7-10   Budget

Expenses:

Poet fees (3 × $1,500)	$4,500
Transportation Expenses	3,000
Facility/Auditorium	600
Posters/Brochures	2,000
Postage/Mailing	585
Staff/Professional Assistance	
Public Relations (30 hours × $30/hr)	900
Coordinator (60 hours × $30/hr)	1,800
Clerical (120 hours × $15/hr)	1,800
Receptions	900
Total Expenses:	**$16,085**

You may want to include in-kind support in both expenses & revenue.

In-kind support might include:

- Promotion on radio stations

- Ticket sales in bookstores

- Food, beverages provided for reception

- Printing (if printer donates service)

FIGURE 7-11   Evaluation Work Sheet

1. Summary of program or service:

a. Actual results:

_____

_____

_____

_____

b. Tickets sold, by category:

_____

_____

_____

_____

c. Revenue generated:

_____

_____

_____

_____

2. Problem areas:

_____

_____

_____

_____

BIBLIOGRAPHY

The AMA Handbook of Marketing for the Service Industries. Carole A. Congram, editor. New York: American Management Association, 1991.

Breen, George Edward, and Albert B. Blankenship. *Do-It-Yourself Marketing Research.* 3rd ed. New York: McGraw-Hill, 1989.

"Journal of Marketing," 55 (1972). Chicago: American Marketing Association.

Kotler, Philip. *Principles of Marketing.* 3rd ed. Englewood Cliffs, N.J.: Prentice-Hall, 1986.

Kotler, Philip, and Gary Armstrong. *Principles of Marketing.* 4th ed. Englewood Cliffs, N.J.: Prentice-Hall, 1989.

Kotler, Philip, and L. R. Eduardo. *Social Marketing: Strategies for Changing Public Behavior.* New York: The Free Press, 1989.

Kotler, Philip, et al. *The New Competition.* Englewood Cliffs, N.J.: Prentice-Hall, 1985.

Lauffer, Armand. *Strategic Marketing for Not-for-Profit Organizations: Program and Resource Development.* New York: The Free Press, 1984.

Levitt, Theodore. *The Marketing Imagination.* New York: The Free Press, 1986.

Lord, James Gregory. *Philanthropy and Marketing: New Strategies for Fund Raising.* Cleveland: Third Sector Press, 1981.

Lovelock, Christopher H., and Charles B. Weinberg. *Marketing for Public and Nonprofit Managers.* New York: Wiley, 1984.

Luther, William M. *The Marketing Plan, How to Prepare & Implement It.* New York: AMACOM, American Management Association, 1982.

McKenna, Regis. *Relationship Marketing: Successful Strategies for the Age of the Customer.* Reading, Mass.: Addison-Wesley Publishing, 1991.

Nichols, Judith E. *By the Numbers: Using Demographics and Psychographics for Business Growth in the '90s.* Chicago: Bonus Books, 1990.

Rados, David L. *Marketing for Non-Profit Organizations.* Boston: Auburn House Publishing, 1981.

Ries, Al and Jack Trout. *Positioning: The Battle For Your Mind.* New York: McGraw-Hill, 1981.

Rodgers, F.G. "Buck," with Robert L. Shook. *The IBM Way: Insights Into the World's Most Successful Marketing Organization.* New York: Harper & Row, 1986.

Simons, Robin, et al. *Nonprofit Piggy Goes to Market: How the Denver Children's Museum Earns $600,000 Annually.* Denver, Colo.: The Children's Museum of Denver, 1984.

Steckel, Dr. Richard, with Robin Simons and Peter Langsfelder. *Filthy Rich & Other Nonprofit Fantasies: Changing the way nonprofits do business in the 90's.* Berkeley, Calif.: Ten Speed Press, 1989.

Templeton, Jane Farley. *Focus Groups: A Guide for Marketing & Advertising Professionals.* Chicago: Probus Publishing Company, 1987.

Tull, Donald S., and Del I. Hawkins. *Marketing Research: Measurement and Method.* 3rd ed., New York: Macmillan Publishing, 1984.

INDEX

Suzanne Walters is president of Walters & Associates, Strategic Marketing Development Consultants, in Denver, Colorado. She was previously the Director of Marketing for the Denver Public Library. During her tenure, marketing and customer service programs resulted in a $91.6 million bond election victory, making it possible to build a new central library and to build and renovate branches throughout the city.

Book design: Gloria Brown
Cover design: Apicella Design
Typography: Maryland Composition Company, Inc.